Oh, Lord, It's
MONDAY
Again

Esther Blumenfeld and Lynne Alpern
Illustrated by Cal Warlick

PEACHTREE PUBLISHERS, LTD.
Atlanta

Published by
PEACHTREE PUBLISHERS, LTD.
494 Armour Circle, NE
Atlanta, GA 30324

Design by Candace J. Magee
Composition by Kathryn D. Mothershed

Manufactured in the United States of America

10 9 8 7 6 5 4 3 2 1

Library of Congress Cataloging in Publication Data

Blumenfeld, Esther.
      Oh, Lord, it's Monday again / Esther Blumenfeld and Lynne Alpern ; illustrated by Cal Warlick.
         p. cm.
      ISBN 1-56145-026-X (pbk.) : $6.95
      1. Business--Humor. 2. Work--Humor. I. Alpern, Lynne.
II. Title.
PN6231.B85B54   1991
818'.5402080355--dc20

91-16675
CIP

Dedication

Other books

by Esther Blumenfeld and Lynne Alpern:

Oh, Lord, I Sound Just Like Mama

In-Laws, Outlaws & Other Theories of Relativity

Mama's Cooking: Celebrities Remeber Mama's Best Recipe

The Smile Connection: How to Use Humor in Dealing with People

For: Those summers I spent in the trouser factory so I could afford college,
For: Those various schools where I served hard time as an attendance counselor and schoolmarm,
For: Warren and Josh, who keep me in odd jobs, and
For: All the editors who gave me the business.

Thanks!
Esther Blumenfeld

To my favorite bosses:
My dad, Julian Shapiro, for introducing me to writs, deeds, and Percy Foreman;
Marion Collier, the only manager who ever let me take a five minute typing test in ten minutes;
Bob, Eve, and Ken, for expanding my job description; and Betty Stein, a medical librarian who knows what dedication is all about.

Lynne Alpern

Acknowledgments

A special note of thanks to our editors at *Business Atlanta,* past and present, for giving us free rein to color outside the lines, and to Les Kirschbaum of Mid-Continent Agencies, Norm and Helene Oleesky of C&C Hardware and Ruth Shapiro, for having more than their share of funny moments at work;

And our deepest appreciation to our seriously funny Peachtree editors, Margaret Quinlin and Susan Thurman; a master illustrator, Cal Warlick; our gifted photographer, Nancy Maxwell Goldberg; dynamos Kathy Landwehr, Jill Smith, Candace Magee, and Faye Smallwood; and all the other devoted and hardworking folks at Peachtree who left their incriminating fingerprints on this book.

Esther & Lynne

TABLE OF CONTENTS

Introduction

Your boss's secretary quits, so he hires yours. You catch the file clerk humming cheerfully while measuring the floor space around your typewriter. Your biggest customer cancels his order because he is hopping a one-way flight to Pago-Pago.

As Queen Isabella said to Ferdinand when Christopher Columbus asked for more doubloons, "Oh, Lord, it's Monday again."

Whether you have just survived your first Monday on the job, or you're a seasoned veteran in the trenches, you're likely to encounter many adventures as you tiptoe gingerly down that 130,000 hour path toward retirement. And you are going to meet up with several co-workers whose little quirks will liven up your day.

You know you've survived another wacky day at work when your stapler is missing, an alien liverwurst sandwich is turning green in your wastebasket, and your favorite ballpoint pen is decorated with the teethmarks of a stranger.

Elbert Hubbard said, "Life is just one damn thing after another." Your colleagues who have embellished these pages with their true stories and witticisms know this, and they are in cahoots with us as we unravel the mysteries of the 9-5 world.

As correspondents on the business scene for many years, we thought we'd seen it all. Our first editor at *Business Atlanta* magazine slept on a bed of nails and ate writers for lunch. When we proposed a humor column, he barked, "Nothing makes me laugh, but give it a shot. If it works, fine. If not — you're out."

After reading our piece about business jargon called "Funeralizing the Mother Tongue," his own tongue stopped flapping long enough to crack open the monthly "Coffeebreak" column for us. And for several years thereafter, we turned over every rock in BusinessLand's well-landscaped garden looking for more funny grub.

We've explored the follies of the workday world from "A Picnic with your Co-workers is NO Picnic " to "It's Hard to Pull Yourself Up by the Bootstraps When You're Naked." Fun it's been, and more. Through fiscal fiascos, bear markets, and a lot of bull, laughter makes the good times better and the bad times bearable.

But we knew it was time for this book, after we wrote a book review parody on the non-existent *How To Lose Customers and Antagonize Them For Life,* by Manfred MacAbre for Flummery Press. This "book" must have hit a nerve, because the editors at *Business Atlanta* were swamped with calls from readers asking where they could buy the book. One frantic secretary phoned and said, "I've scoured every store in the city, and my boss told me not to come back without it." So to save her job, we decided to write this book.

Mabel, you can go back to work now.

P.S. If **Oh, Lord, It's MONDAY Again** calls up some funny moments from your memory database, we'd love to hear from you the old-fashioned way, if not today, MONDAY, at Box 14413, Atlanta, GA 30324.

CHAPTER 1

My Boss Can Suck the Sunshine Out of Any Day in Thirty Seconds Flat

(Day-to-Day with Your Co-Workers Is NO Picnic)

The company picnic is becoming trendy in many businesses. Inviting their employees out to the local park, bosses reinforce the "we-are-one-big-happy-family" concept.

So to ensure successful picnics, many firms are now hiring experts to turn what used to be a haphazard event into a new organizational tradition. To wit . . .

MEMORANDUM TO: Staff
FROM: The President of OMNIBUX Inc.
I'm sure you will all be delighted to know that we have hired an outside consultant to analyze the results of last year's company picnic. Dr. Merton Bagatelle is an expert in group dynamics, specializing in The Power Lunch. Please afford him your utmost cooperation, as he will be in charge of structuring this year's event.

TO: All Department Heads
FROM: Merton Bagatelle
I have not yet received any of the questionnaires concerning my picnic performance appraisal study, which I asked you to distribute to your department. Please ensure that these answer sheets are returned to me immediately so I can make a statistical

analysis of the results. I can assure you this year's picnic will not be left to spontaneity.

TO: All Department Personnel
FROM: The Head of Quality Control
Will the employee who put 167 picnic questionnaires in the tissue dispensers in the men's bathroom next to Dr. Bagatelle's office, please see me?

TO: Merton Bagatelle
FROM: Bookkeeping Department
RE: Picnic Games Committee
Our thinking on the three-legged race is that it should be eliminated this year since none of our women want to be tied to Mr. Sidney, head of Order Handling, ever again.

TO: Bookkeeping Department
FROM: Merton Bagatelle
RE: Games Committee
I will go along with your suggestion to eliminate Mr. Sidney and the three-legged race. However, this year I must insist that Vice President Norton be assigned to the Blue volleyball team, since neither side chose him last year.

Also, if the picnic is to be held at the dairy again this year, the Competitive Analysis Department wants the softball game located further away from the cowpen. Furthermore, several people suggested that the traditional cow-milking event has lost its appeal after last year's contest, when our night watchman mistook Clarence for Rosebud.

TO: Audio Visual/Training Department
FROM: Merton Bagatelle
Am sending along a new training film, "Company Picnics and How They Got That Way." If you start now, separating each company division into groups of twelve, we can train everyone properly in correct picnic procedures in the four weeks remaining before The Big Event.

Each quality control circle will then evaluate and implement adaptations of the film. Topics covered are: "Time and Motion Studies of Departmental Games," "Acceptable Boss-vs.-Employee Territorial Perspectives in Open Spaces," and "Personnel Deployment for Optimum Tug-of-war Competition." Included also is the animated short, "How to Tell Cows from Bulls without Embarrassment."

TO: Audio Visual/Training Department
FROM: Merton Bagatelle
There seems to be some confusion about what happened to my training film. I trust there is no relationship to its turning up missing the same day the smoke alarms went off in your offices. Please keep me informed.

```
TO:       Staff
FROM:     Department of Traffic and Transportation
RE:       Cooking Spaces Reserved for Executive Hibachis
```
In accordance with Dr. Bagatelle's recommendation, please observe new space allocations. The president, all vice presidents, and members of the board may use cooking outlets at the pavilion overlooking the lake.

Supervisors, managers, and production foremen are assigned to marked spaces adjacent to the boat docks. All others can park their barbecue grills alphabetically on the concrete slab near the hogpen.

```
CONFIDENTIAL TO:  All Department Heads
FROM:     Merton Bagatelle
```
Please advise employees that it will be considered in poor taste to ask the company president or members of the board if our comptroller will get out of Folsom Prison in time for this year's picnic.

TO BE POSTED ON ALL BULLETIN BOARDS
(By authorization of Merton Bagatelle):
***LOOK FOR THE SURPRISE CELEBRITY GUEST
AT THIS YEAR'S PICNIC!***

INTERNAL MEMO TO: All Employees
FROM: Public Relations
We deeply regret to announce the death of the founder of our
company, J. D. Muggenrun, who at 98 was still a driving force
and inspiration to us all.

Funeral Parlor: Muggenrun Funeral Home, Muggenrun Island,
Maine.   Funeral service: 10:15 a.m. in Hepplewhite Chapel.

The newspaper accounts of Mr. Muggenrun's sudden demise in the
presence of an exotic dancer—known for balancing frozen
daiquiris on her forty-two-inch bosom—were greatly exaggerated.
Damage control will portray the event as a field study of glass
equilibrium on wobbly surfaces.

TO: All Department Heads
FROM: Merton Bagatelle
Does anyone have a suggestion for a surprise celebrity guest
replacement for this year's picnic?   Please contact me
immediately.

TO: All Employees
FROM: Information Systems
Due to a computer malfunction, we will be unable to distribute
the detailed picnic maps to any of the 1,671 employees before
Saturday. If you need directions, we are sure Dr. Bagatelle will
be happy to answer your questions.   All of them.

```
TO:       Personnel Director
FROM:     Merton Bagatelle
RE:       Food Committee
```

I received your memo about the warning signs of the binding forces of a new ideology, the web of belongingness, and company goals vs. individual goals. Could you please explain what all this has to do with the picnic food committee?

```
TO:       Merton Bagatelle
FROM:     Personnel Director
```

Bookkeeping's Serenity Pickens, whom you appointed to chair the food committee, is a full-blown humanistic vegetarian, and the picnic menu now consists of what the cows grazed on last year.

```
TO:       Serenity Pickens
FROM:     Merton Bagatelle
```

In light of the cancellation of the three-legged race, Mr. Sidney, head of Order Handling, has eagerly consented to co-chair the food committee with you.

```
TO:       Serenity Pickens
FROM:     Personnel Director
```

I just read Dr. Bagatelle's announcement of your resignation from the food committee. For my part, I shall certainly miss you and do hope you leave with only minor regrets.

TO: Merton Bagatelle
FROM: Mr. Sidney
I ordered peanut butter, paper cups, and daiquiri mix. Now what?

TO: All Employees
FROM: Merton Bagatelle
Sign-up sheets will be distributed for this year's potluck picnic to be held in the company parking lot.

URGENT: TO BE POSTED IMMEDIATELY ON ALL BULLETIN BOARDS
FROM: The President's Office
PICNIC CANCELLED BECAUSE OF RAIN.

P.S. For those employees wishing to send cards or visit Merton Bagatelle, visiting hours at Parkwell Psychiatric Hospital are from 2-4 p.m. We know you join us in wishing him well and hope that he will recover in time to plan our upcoming Christmas party.

Day-to-day with Your Co-workers Is NO Picnic

I'm going to put "Do Not Disturb" on my tombstone just to see if that will work.

MBAs are extremely sensitive about being underpaid.

My supervisor is responsible for three departments, seventy-five employees and five peptic ulcers.

You know you are facing a deadline when some fool sticks his face in your office and asks, "Working hard?"

The one woman on our board has learned that more vital decisions have been made standing at adjoining urinals than sitting in the boardroom.

Yesterday my secretary complained, "You give me so much work I don't have time to do my personal stuff!"

I have an employee with an attitude problem. He resents work.

The Japanese say your business should be like one big family. That's what I come to work to get away from.

Exactly how much honesty is an employee expected to take?

The most gratifying words a company president can hear are "THANKS, DAD."

EVEN WHEN YOU'RE AN INFLUENTIAL BANKER in Dallas, it's hard to be impressive when you walk into your new client's office and his grey-haired secretary exclaims, "Well, if it isn't little Georgie Mayer! Get over here, boy, and give me a hug!"

For a year now we've wanted to fire our incompetent office manager, but she's the best pitcher our softball team ever had.

There's nothing written in the company by-laws that says the president has to make any sense.

You know you're in trouble when you're invited to your boss's home for dinner, you break a crystal goblet, and no one says, "Oh, don't worry, it's OK."

I was named Employee-of-the-Month for figuring out a tactful way to eliminate the Employee-of-the-Month award.

My attitude toward my job improved when I quit.

An unsuccessful partnership is like a harp. After the song has been plucked, the strings are still there.

My company has a formal salary review program. They serve you tea and politely say, "No."

Every boss should get down on his knees and clean under the rim of a toilet bowl at least once a year.

The garment business used to run on a pat formula. Now it's called sexual harassment.

He is the most dynamically ineffective salesman in my department.

Giving everybody a raise makes everybody happy except the chuckleheads who really earned it.

I'd be lost without my partner. It's so convenient to have someone else to blame.

Wherever there are employees with idle teenagers, you'll find a beleaguered personnel director under summer siege.

When a business full of quiet, understated folks hires a raucous, slap-'em-on-the-back salesman, the gears are going to grind.

I notified my customer service rep that wearing his dentures is part of the dress code.

Most workers want to like their work so it would
be considerate of the boss to come up with a reason.

Ten-to-one, if a guy blames his secretary for his mistakes, he also underpays her.

The quietest dinner party I ever gave was when I accidentally seated my boss next to his ex-wife's lawyer.

It's DIFFICULT TO CONCENTRATE when the president of your company gets murdered on vacation, his flashy second wife is the prime suspect, and she shows up Monday morning to criticize your sales report.

Chapter 2

Funeralizing the Mother Tongue
(Jargon and Other Communication Capers)

Several years ago Leo Aikman wrote about seeing a Bell Telephone truck which had "Ask Me About Better Telephone Service" painted on its door. Underneath someone had scribbled in the dust, "I don't talk to no trucks." We felt it was time to track down the linguistic critic who scrawled those defiant words and located self-made businessman, George Fenster, in his office at OmniBux, Inc.

"Mr. Fenster, what about your graffiti in the dust?" His reaction surprised us. "I'd have been better off talking to the truck. I used to get straight talk from folks. But not now. I've got as much of a fat chance as a slim one of understanding people nowadays. It's that damn jargon."

"What do you mean?"

"For instance, my stockbroker called me Friday and said that when she saw that double bottom, she thought about my spread and suggested I lift a leg. I didn't know if she was advising me or talking dirty."

Leaning intently across the desk, he added, "That's not all. Then my wife, Martha, and I had the family over for Sunday supper. None of us could understand each other. I asked my nephew, Basil, to fix my TV. After five years at MIT, he should be able to do something."

"And did he?"

"Yes, but not before he informs me that my TV malfunctions because 'an alien electro-magnetic field is interfering with the normal raster scan of the directed electron gun.'"

"Why didn't he just come plain out and say that someone left a stereo speaker sitting on your set?"

"When I asked him that, he apologized for not taking my socio-emotional needs into account. I made him wash his mouth out with soap! Then my niece, Tiffany Marie, tells us they are doing assets stripping at her company. That upset Martha, since she's been reading about that sexual harassment stuff. And if that weren't bad enough, Tiffie's realtor told her that she couldn't buy the house she had bid on because there was some gazumping going on."

"It must have been quite an evening."

"Yes, and it really got rolling when our son, Baxter, told a joke in Fortran. When he bought his computer, I asked him to teach me about that dang-blasted machine. But I'll never do that again."

"What happened?"

"He tells me, 'the cpu via the user-input device has scanned a value which does not conform to an established ASCII protocol stored within the system bios.'"

"What does that mean?"

"It means I hit the wrong key!"

At that moment Fenster's able secretary Smythe entered with some urgent messages. Fenster asked us to wait while Smythe relayed the information.

"First, from the Director of Human Resources Planning: 'Mailroom employee, Beasley Frobnitz, has been phased out, due to negative patient-care outcome. Human interment space has been reserved at Sprinkledowns, and Frobnitz will be funeralized at 0-900, Monday morning.'" Fenster's cheek began twitching.

"Next, a memo from OmniBux Security: 'There will be a fire drill tomorrow afternoon. Employees on C Hall will ingress the doors marked STAIRWELL TO B. This will give more flexibility in case of rapid oxidation. However, in case of energetic disassembly, employees on D should interface with workers from C, egressing at the exit marked EMERGENCY EXIT G, DO NOT ENTER. An access controller will let you out once you've reached the bottom floor.'" Fenster's face reddened.

"Finally, from Bronsky in the typing pool: 'Having prioritized available funding, your request for a staff-support facilitator cannot be actuated at present. However, sustain interliaisation, because new game plan capabilities will include strict concerns for programming a more successful situation to direct a most maximally impactful plan for future manpowerization.'"

Clutching his throat, Fenster exploded with system overload. "Smythe, what the hell does that mean?"

"Well, sir, I think it means you can't get that temporary typist you requested for the day I'm having my non-vital teeth removed." Fenster managed only a weak wave as we left him tangled in a morass of buzzwords.

Is the world of work really sinking in a mire of verbal garbage? Moishe Hayakawa, Yale Professor of Obfuscation and Linguistic Engineering, claims "there's a pony in there somewhere. It's bad, but not hopeless.

And a Certified Linguistic Engineer like Hayakawa could easily tackle the problem: "When you really get down to it, what merits more study is not so much the various ways by which alien agents of disequilibrium infiltrate phonological systems, as what happens once maximal differentiation peaks. Need I say more?"

No. Please no.

Jargon and Other Communication Capers

If it sounds good and doesn't make any sense, it's jargon.

Accounts receivable. If only they were.

A smart PR director can downgrade a disaster into a crisis.

"Refine your assumptions" means "Guess again."

If Shakespeare were alive today, he'd write, "Alas, poor Yorick, he's been downsized."

"That goes without saying." Would that he had!

SINCE I NEVER REMEMBER NAMES, I made a special effort at a party to remember the name of the young woman sitting next to me. When my wife joined us, I triumphantly introduced them. My wife laughed, "Steve, what are you doing? You just introduced me to my own secretary."

Customers feel a moral duty to complain, whereas employees do it just for the hell of it.

"Counter-intuitive" means "What a dumb idea."

When my boss talks, I keep waiting for a period, but all he gives me are commas.

"She is eager to learn" really means, "She'll drive you nuts."

When your lawyer starts talking Latin, call a priest.

Chrysler lays off five thousand workers and calls it "initiating a career alternative enhancement program."

It isn't that my partner won't meet me halfway. It's just that he's such a lousy judge of distance.

✎   ✏

WHEN MY BUSINESS PARTNER FROM AUSTRALIA moved to New York, she had a terrible time adjusting to American slang. One morning waiting for her breakfast order in a diner, the counter man smiled at her and hollered, "Toasted English muffin!" Highly insulted, she yelled, "Bloody bloke!" and marched out.

✎

Abandoning my briefcase causes me separation anxiety.

"Our CEO retired gracefully" means,
"we didn't have to carry him out
kicking and screaming."

"I doubt the implementation of your plan" really means, "There's no chance in hell it will work."

If your boss says you can call her by her first name, it's a sure sign you're not getting the raise.

Boom and bust, bear and bull, inflation and deflation . . . ah, what a better place the world would be without antonyms.

My secretary likes to play with words and often loses.

The job description never includes "dingbat assistant."

If you want to instill confidence in your new client, quit talking about playing with his money.

A CUSTOMER IN CALIFORNIA with a bill long overdue phoned to say, "The check is in the mail." Immediately he screamed, "It's an earthquake and, my God, the ground has split wide open and swallowed the mailbox—with your check in it!"

When the new "whiz kid" hits me with an idea, I always say, "I'll think about it." I don't say for how long.

It's easier to communicate if you don't have much to say.

Personnel directors love small talk. It makes them think you like them.

The newfangled phone in my office makes it easier than ever to find new and creative ways to look stupid.

"Good morning," I said to the merchant in Istanbul, "how much is that rug?"
"Two thousand dollars."
"I'll give you one thousand."
"I'll take eighteen hundred."
"I'll give you nine hundred."
"No, no, you don't understand," cried the Turkish trader. "When I come down, you go up!"
"Oh, sorry. Let's try again. How much is that rug?"
"Two thousand dollars."
"I'll give you one thousand."
"I'll take sixteen hundred."
"I'll give you eight hundred."
"NO NO! I go down, you go UP! Please try once more."
"OK, sorry. How much is that rug?"
"Two thousand dollars."
"I'll give you one thousand dollars."
"SOLD!"

CHAPTER 3

Oh, Lord, It's **MONDAY** Again

(Notes on the Paper Trail)

"**M**oses, take a note."

When God dictated the Ten Commandments to Moses and told him to lug those sixty-one pounds of stone down from Mount Sinai, even He could not have predicted how the world's first memos would go forth and multiply. Over the years, the weight of memos gradually shifted from the medium to the message.

Not at first, of course. Ancient executives thought long and hard before dashing off subsequent memos that took weeks to chisel out of granite ("To all members of the Tigris-Euphrates Longshoremen's Union: Please hack out your name after you've read this memo and drag it over to the next person on the list").

When too many scribes began succumbing to memo-carver's elbow, business leaders experimented with other vehicles to disperse semi-vital information. Independently, cultures around the globe tried carrier pigeons, wandering minstrels, smoke signals, and even town criers. Alas, the time lag sabotaged many a committee meeting, if the message got through at all.

Johann Gutenberg changed all that. With the invention of movable type in the fifteenth century, he unleashed an avalanche of paper that has finally come to rest at the feet of computer technology. Yo, PC.

In those crucial intervening centuries, however, memos begat memos, and "memo-talk" confused the unwary recipients. Company employees from the president to the receptionist sent memos to announce new products, commemorate birthdays, chastise sales departments, jockey for position, outmaneuver the competition, and cover their tracks. The logging industry boomed and creativity crept into the world of words.

Tell the truth. When your office door closes, what do you really do with that mountain of memos? Some view an impressive stack as a measure of popularity, and a few speedreading honor graduates even read them. Confessed memo exterminators, however, admit to dropping them behind file cabinets, using them as coffee cup blotters and even smuggling them out of the office for external disposal. Ever wonder what's in those bulging briefcases?

If the lost art of writing short, readable memos is ever revived, it will re-surface on a computer screen. Voice mail, electronic messaging, Telex, fax machines, and in-house computer networks are making the printed memo as extinct as the wooly mammoth. And the smart executive will get a jump on the antique market by squirreling away memos likely to become valuable in future decades.

Anticipating a burgeoning flea market bonanza, we interviewed Duke University Memo-tion expert, Dr. Waterman Hurley, about accumulating wealth through collecting memos. Here's the Hurley Method for evaluating your memos for investment and re-sale potential in the dot matrix years to come.

The basic impersonal memo, a photocopied form letter, is worth . . . absolutely nothing. An original memo, typed on white vellum, currently sells for one dollar. Add seventy-five cents for a vice-president's signature in real ink (not ballpoint).

If your memo is slightly tattered, halve the value. If it's been folded, spindled, or mutilated in a momentary fit of anger, the value plummets to thirteen cents. But don't worry. The real money is in commemorative memos, matched sets, mint sets, and first day of issue memos.

Any memo received before 1923 is already considered an antique. Those from cannibalized or extinct companies are highly prized. So a really old manager should be sure to hang onto a 1910 Gimbel's presidential memo.

Limited editions are also worth saving. A limited edition memo is one received from a CEO on the job for less than three months. Designer originals (handwritten), currently worth $8.62, are also a goldmine. Coffee rings, doodles, and fingerprints increase its value—anything showing the touch of an actual live person.

Celebrity memos from any supervisor (Orville Redenbacher, for instance) who later became famous are always popular. If the person went to jail or appeared in the *National Enquirer,* the value triples. Equally valuable will be the last printed memo ever written. But most desirable of all, for which memo hounds have hunted unsuccessfully for years, for which Sotheby's already has a bid of $294,000, and the real reason Dr. Livingston went to Africa, is also the most rare: a clear, concise memo.

Thou shalt search in vain.

Notes on the Paper Trail

At our next committee meeting, the discussion will be a continuation of our last discussion on the same topic and a decision will be made when to hold further discussion.

It's scary when your kid's resume is better than yours.

When I lost my pocket diary, I lost a year of my life.

Impromptu meetings are better when they're planned out ahead of time.

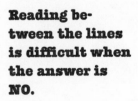

Thank God my customer decided not to FAX me his invoice because his cat threw up into his FAX machine.

Reading between the lines is difficult when the answer is NO.

My secretary's "in" box is labeled "routinely urgent."

On my first job as a secretary, I made so many typing errors that I spent my whole first paycheck on a briefcase to smuggle out my nine pounds of mistakes at the end of each day.

The way to write a captivating memo is leave out the parts that people skip.

The only thing my boss ever physically writes himself is his name, and that's illegible.

FAX a new joke to a customer in Yonkers and twenty minutes later it will come back to you as an old one from Walla Walla.

If your memos are succinct and perfectly clear, you're not ready to write a position paper.

It takes a three-hundred-page print-out to spit out the one number I need.

DOCTORS COMPLAIN ABOUT INSURANCE. Lawyers complain about briefs. Professors complain about manuscripts. Nurses complain about charts. Scientists complain about reports. Salespeople complain about invoices. The only person I know who's still happy with his job is our accountant, and she works for all of them.

After getting a busy signal at my branch office for forty-five minutes, I sent my manager a FAX: "Get off the phone!"

If it's in a memo, it's not your fault.

Everything Voltaire wrote he read to his cook. If she didn't understand it, he rewrote it. Where's Voltaire's cook now that we really need her?

Perspective brings the ability to re-read my proposal and ask, "What fool put this in?"

You want to eliminate unnecessary paperwork? Bring back the mimeograph machine.

If you want people to remember you, insist that last month's minutes be read aloud.

My mother, the high-powered, tough-talking international lawyer, stashes all her "to do's" in a file labeled "Dis 'n Dat."

It's easy to stay in shape when you're bench-pressing stacks of insurance forms an hour after quitting time.

If you don't want to talk to someone, ask him to put it in a memo so you can put off ignoring him 'til later.

Today is the deadline for responses to my memo. The new deadline is next Friday.

Why is it no one thinks I can figure out they've sent me something without attaching a memo that tells me they've sent it?

More bang for your bucks? This note was posted in the men's room of the College of Business Administration at a large university:

Will anyone finding a .38 revolver please turn it in at the security office.

Sincerely,
Officer Mulrooney

CHAPTER 4

Who Wants Financial Advice from a Spotted Mackerel?

(Consultants and Other Experts)

"**W**hy does my beagle howl when he hears Sam Donaldson on TV?"

"How do I deal with a brother-in-law who falls asleep every time I tell a joke?"

"If the government can lower the deficit by $1.5 billion by coming up with two sets of statistics on the same day, why can't I do the same thing with my income tax return?"

Everyone has questions. And every day the local newspaper provides answers. For a mere twenty-five cents a day (fifty cents for advice imported from New York City) you can find—along with all the news that's fit to print and much that isn't—unlimited advice on how to run your life.

No question is too silly or too complicated for pundits of the press to ponder. But before following a recommendation to liquify portfolios or slap your poodle and/or brother-in-law with a rolled-up newspaper, ask two questions: Who are these purveyors of influence so free with their counsel? And after following un-workable advice, can I get my twenty-five cents back?

As for the twenty-five cents, the publisher can always claim that you probably got your money's worth from the rest of the paper. Better, perhaps, to concentrate instead on the qualifications of the "expert" columnists before you consider acting on their words.

Often the small print at the bottom of the article offers you a clue. If it says "staff reporter," the writer's only qualification may be that when his editor wanted to start a gardening column and asked, "Who knows something about mulching?" he was the unfortunate one who made eye contact. In that case, you can only hope the writer is playing with all his equipment on a level field.

There are, of course, credentials even more impressive than "editorial staff," such as M.D., psychologist, attorney, or former CEO of a prestigious company. Caveat emptor!

Keeping in mind 50 percent of all professionals graduated in the bottom half of their class, it would be helpful to know a dermatologist's class standing before following her prescription to wrap your face in grape leaves. Also, does the psychologist who tells parents to reason with their two-year-old have any children? And if your own attorney charges fifty dollars for a telephone opinion, how can the lawyer/columnist afford to give verdicts away?

Or when a cardiologist advises readers to drop thirty pounds, stop smoking cold turkey and relax, is the cardiologist a fingernail biter? If credentials state "former CEO," isn't it legitimate to wonder why he is no longer with the firm? On the other hand, if he is touted as president of Omnibux Inc., will credits reveal the business was inherited last week from dotty Aunt Matilda? If "Miss Etiquette" tells you to eat octopus tentacles in pairs only, is her ink dry? And don't you have a right to know?

Economists are another story altogether. An economist awakens in the morning with the answer and spends all day figuring out the question. Is something perfectly clear? That's when a gaggle of economic experts will step in to confuse you with the economic two-step such as, "Absence of data on the potential problem can only lead to speculation at this time." If the economist didn't know, why did he take up so much space?

So what makes an authority? Why not try it ourselves? After all, Laurence Peter, author of *The Peter Principle* said, "Make three correct guesses consecutively and you will establish a reputation as an expert."

Therefore we submit these three guesses for success:

1. Keep your mind on business.
2. Use your head today.
3. A mistake can teach you a valuable lesson.

Voila! We now qualify as expert advice givers, who offer professional advice to the following questions (keep in mind this advice is already worth $6.95, which makes it twenty-eight times better already):

QUESTION: I am in charge of office collections. How do I get people to give?

ANSWER: Threaten to wipe an oily rag over their computer screens.

QUESTION: I have the job my boss used to have. He knows how little work it takes because he used to do it. And I know how little work it takes to do my former job, but none of us can say anything because we will all be exposed. What should I do?

ANSWER: You pretend to work and management will pretend to pay you. It all works out.

QUESTION: My wife left me two years ago. Recently I inherited $1 million. She wants a reconciliation. Do I need a lawyer?

ANSWER: You need to decide if you want to share your wealth with your wife or your lawyer. Have you ever considered marrying your lawyer? You might consolidate your losses.

QUESTION: After reading all the columns in my paper, I'm confused. Whose advice should I take?

ANSWER: Presume everyone is wrong. You can't lose.

Consultants and Other Experts

If you're going to be a perfectionist, at least charge by the hour.

You know it's a consultant when his sales call becomes an "initial diagnostic interview."

Last week I was sent to a whole brain workshop led by a half-wit.

Most economic forecasts are almost close to being right in a relative sense.

My daughter not only graduated from Harvard Business School, she managed to get over it.

There's nothing worse than being trapped in morning traffic with my carpool, no air-conditioning, and a dang-blasted motivational tape.

When your son, the new stockbroker, calls with a hot tip, a wise parent will bypass the transaction and just mail him a check for the commission.

Want to see the consultant get jumpy? Take a course in his specialty.

Who needs competence when you've got expertise?

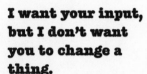

I want your input, but I don't want you to change a thing.

✏ ✏ ✏

MEDICAL LIBRARIANS KNOW ACCURACY CAN SAVE LIVES. Thus when an orthopedic intern asked me, "How many men are rejected by the army because of flat feet?" I spent three hours tracking down the answer for her. That night my husband, also an intern, said, "Did you know 5 percent of all army recruits get turned down for flat feet? I bet Georganne, the new intern, it was 10 percent, but she disagreed. Honey, I hope you're not upset that I lost five dollars."

✏ ✏

Rub two accountants together and you'll get Chapter 11.

The more significant your boo-boos, the more pretentious the law firm.

Four months of training qualifies a stockbroker to buy, sell, and mangle your money.

Never do business with a man whose office plants are dead.

If you are going to write a time management book the first sentence should not be, "Don't waste your time on things of marginal value."

These days financial horse sense suffers from hoof and mouth disease.

You know the speech will be boring when the subject is motivation.

The first thing to remember when you're selling chicken feed is that you're not selling it to the chickens.

I don't mind when my lawyer asks me a question, but I do mind when he answers himself and then tells me I don't know what I'm talking about.

All I want from my consultants is written reports. If they hang around to implement, I'll never get anywhere.

Often the hardest question to answer is, "Exactly what do you do?"

IF you think things are a mess now,
wait until they send in the guys From
corporate headquarters to Fix it.

WHEN ASKED WHY SO MANY MORE WOMEN than men entrepreneurs started new businesses in the 1990s, marketing professor Ken Bernhardt answers, "Man's best friend is his dog. Woman's best friend are diamonds. Who's smarter?"

When our accounting department meets the auditors, it's calculators at twenty paces.

Experts like to huddle together with similar statistics, so no authority on the subject looks ridiculous all by himself.

AS A LABOR ARBITRATOR, being locked in a motel room with opposing sides is uncomfortable enough. But on one occasion the air in the room was so thick with smoke that I finally said, "Do you mind not smoking for a while?" Soon deciding to take a caucus, both sides left the room and returned shortly.

"We have come to an agreement, Mr. Arbitrator. We don't think someone who is supposed to arbitrate a tobacco company should ask us to quit smoking. You are dismissed."

CHAPTER 5

How to Lose Customers and Antagonize Them for Life

(Customer Relations)

HOW TO LOSE CUSTOMERS & ANTAGONIZE THEM FOR LIFE, by Manfred MacAbre. *(Flummery Press* $19.95)

A customer tasted one of the grapes the fruit vendor had just weighed for her. "Pardon me," she complained, "but I asked for seedless grapes." The lines in the vendor's face tightened. Grabbing the cluster of grapes, he shook them in her face. "So what's the matter, lady," he barked, "you can't spit out?"

The uneasy truce between merchants and customers has finally ended. And according to author Manfred MacAbre, the trickle-down theory of built-in customer obsolescence relates directly to the takeover movement of publicly-owned American corporations in the l980s. Mergers have at long last made the customer redundant—a change well documented in his latest book, *How To Lose Customers & Antagonize Them For Life.*

Management caught in the greed crunch must decide what is good for their shareholders while simultaneously scrambling to protect their precarious positions. So who has time for customers? When corporate raider T. Bone Picker made a two-tier offer for OmniBux Corporation in 1987, he advised their directors, "Liquefy your assets. The money's in the merger, not the goods." Overnight the business climate shifted as shareholders realized that, with buyouts, customers are no longer needed.

MacAbre's argument is compelling: with the borrowed billions it takes for a buyout, a company will have to pay no taxes, due to tax deductible loan interest.

Consequently there is no need for customers, since the cash burden will not allow the company to invest in new products anyway.

As he delves into the customer nuisance factor for the average business, the book becomes a page turner. MacAbre, a former demolitions expert for Donald Trump, carefully documents his strategy for blowing customers out of the water.

Currently, only 68 percent of all customers desert a business because of an indifferent attitude toward them by owners, managers, or employees. But the typical dissatisfied consumer will tell at least ten people about the experience. So consistent mishandling of customers and their orders pays off.

Customer disservice is now the cornerstone of American business. And according to MacAbre's research, the building blocks toward consumer elimination are NO HELP, NO HURRY, NO TRUST, and NO NEED. Sprinkling his trailblazer with colorful vignettes, MacAbre reminds us that generating bad feelings and not solving customer problems work well. As Yogi Berra said, "If people don't want to come out to the ballpark, nobody's gonna stop 'em."

Start with the premise that the customer is not always right, the computer is always right. Few people will argue with machine logic. MacAbre illustrates: "When the customer calls to place an order, the salesperson must first ask the customer for a number . . . any number will do, because the computer will be down." Next, ask the customer to call back. Then, when he hangs up, take the phone off the hook." Customers, MacAbre says, will remember that extra touch from this NO HELP building block.

The author's other building blocks include:

NO TRUST: Sally asks the sixteen-year-old jewelry clerk, "Do you have clip earrings in stock?" and the clerk replies, "I don't think so. It's my first day on the job. But would you like me to pierce your ears?"

NO NEED: "Dear Sir: The company would have recalled your car sooner, but there were so many models without brakes, it took a while to catch up with all their owners."

NO HURRY: Even celebrities fall prey to the consumer elimination plan. The Rev. Billy Graham's plane was grounded due to fog, so he rushed to the railroad station to catch the train for his scheduled appearance. Huffing and puffing, he scurried past the restless line of commuters and asked, "Is this where I get a ticket to Chicago?" "Yes sir, the train is ready to leave now," said the station attendant. Oh, aren't you Dr. Billy Graham?" "Yes, I am," he replied, much relieved. "Can you help me?" "Oh yes," she gushed. "Please step to the end of the line."

The concluding chapter outlines a plan for businesses to contain labor costs while awaiting customer elimination. By convincing customers that they can wait on themselves, management can convert customers into employees and charge them for the privilege.

Research shows, for example, customers will pay to stand in line for their food and then clear their own tables. They will also pay to frame their own pictures, pump their own gas, and zip themselves into designer clothes.

And the company can always answer an occasional complaint with the plausible excuse of the decade: "It's no one's fault, the company has just been sold and is in a state of permanent transition. But we're sure the new owner will address your complaint as soon as we find out who that is . . ."

The book will soon be available in most fish markets, since Flummery Press has just been purchased by Chicken-of-the-Sea.

Customer Relations

I have a standing order with several software salesmen: "Leave me alone!"

There's romance in retail if the customer falls in love with your store.

Small talk is proper before getting down to business. "How's the family?" is not small talk.

You know it's almost closing time when the line is busy and the secretary is not.

A customer called to ask, "Do you have rubbing compound?" I replied, "Yes, what kind do you prefer?" She said, "I have to ask my husband and he isn't home now. Do you have a phone I could call you back on?"

Never order French onion soup at a power lunch unless you carry a Swiss army knife.

There you are, a Harvard MBA in an $800 suit, and your first client calls you "Sonny."

Don't sell anything you wouldn't buy yourself . . . assuming you have good taste.

You want to impress clients? Move into a building with lobby sculpture you don't understand.

How dare you want to buy something that doesn't have a price tag on it?

I'd like more cash and less carry.

The only excuse I ever accepted for an overdue payment came when a check arrived three weeks late with an apology and a crumpled newspaper clipping about a local book-keeper who had been attacked by a rambunctious alligator.

For a banker, a fiduciary relationship is good sex.

I have one supplier who always calls and says, "If you haven't had your aggravation for the day, I'd like a moment of your time."

I worked in mental health for seven years, but I didn't know what genuine paranoia was until I got into real estate.

Strangling your customer is not appropriate body language.

WHEN OUR TV WENT ON THE FRITZ, my mother called our small-town repairman. His wife answered and said they were getting a divorce, but she would relay the message since they were still business partners. Later Mom went to the local diner, where townsfolk greeted her. The TV repairman sat in a booth in the back with two other men. When he spied her, he stood up, waved his arms and yelled across the room, "Hey there, not tonight, Mrs. Richter!"

Call-waiting allows you to insult two clients simultaneously.

The linen service business is like a house of ill-repute. You have it, you sell it, and you still have it.

The first client on your moonlighting job will be your boss's next door neighbor.

When a squirrel fell down her chimney, my favorite customer called my exterminating company, spitting mad. "The dang thing won't stand still long enough for me to get a bead on it with my .38 magnum!"

No one spits on a smiling face.

ONE NIGHT RAY BOLGER, THE FAMOUS DANCER, phoned my friend—a noted French restaurateur—at his home, waking him at midnight to make a lunch reservation. My friend barked at Mr. Bolger, "Call during normal hours!" "Did you hear who I am?" yelled Bolger, "Who are you to be so uppity? I never heard of your restaurant before coming to this town." "That's all right, Mr. Folger," my friend snapped, "I never heard of you either!"

CHAPTER 6

The Case of the Ghost-Written Annual Report

(Research, Creativity and Other Suspicious Behavior)

When was the last time you heard: "That annual report was so spellbinding I couldn't put it down"? Every year corporations spend millions on glossy productions that get tossed out with the leftover beans. Isn't it time these brokers of boredom hired bestselling authors to add some sparkle to their statistics? If they do, perhaps next year's compelling page-turner will look like this one from OmniBux Inc. . .

LIVING, LOVING AND LEVERAGING (To Our Shareholders)
by Leo Buscaglia, the guru of love

The year 1991 ranks as the most fully functioning experience in OmniBux's history. From each separate "I," we the corporation and you the shareholders apportioned space between our onenesses and called it "Us." In this space we have discovered a new intimacy.

Sensitive investors have learned to deal with imperfections and revel in the magic as uncertainty adds spice to corporate life. As we work with holistic intensity to move from an imperfect "then" to a more perfect "now," we are confident 1991 will hold an even greater mystical leap for our customers, employees, and stockholders. Hugs from your CEO.

I, THE TREASURER (Financial Report)
by Mickey Spillane

Debt stinks like a rotting carcass. I discovered the body of assets, now limp and depleted, with red ink oozing from its recently slashed profit margins. Was cutthroat competition responsible? Velda, my leggy blond comptroller, whispered rumors of suffocated acquisitions . . . "bankers" wielding short-term instruments . . . officers enacting statutory (tax) rates.

This year I've witnessed the lifebreath ebb from increasingly dilutive stock options, seen the body of stock ripped asunder by a two-for-one split gone sour. Helpless, I could not prevent the capital offense as inflation strangled growth and choked off funds. I suddenly recalled suspicious overnight borrowing transactions that sucked the life out of loans before maturity. Outside, the river belched up more clues: floating rate notes, floundering debt and sinking fund payments.

Under the gun, I sped back to my office. Snatching the outstanding warrants tacked on my door, I found the final roadblock to redemption of our preferred stock. There on my desk, where disposal of properties had maimed our higher dividend payout ratio, lay our disemboweled portfolio. So who killed profits? Not me, babe.

THE WHAT? (Marketing)
by Dr. Seuss

Rat-a-tat-tategy, it's the marketing strategy,
The world's greatest flim-flam-flattergy of plans.
Mr. Researcher stimulates response by probing friends
For stylish trends.
Targeting men, ladies and even their babies,
He wants to know, WHY? WHY? WHY?
They will BUY, BUY, BUY—or not.
That makes him flop, or flip, or start a-flooping.
Heavens, his idea market can't be drooping!
Hark, it's blooping a bloop.
We've got a scoop—Another zoomer to please the consumer.
And that's the whole poop-a-pooping,
A hoodwink-a-winking.
Just in time to keep our new products from sinking.

NEW PRODUCTS, A CONSERVATIVE VIEW
by William F. Buckley

Pathognomonic to innovation is our commitment to supporting research energumens. With a stable operating environment to minimize at-risk elements, OmniBux's new banking service, Servi-Bux, is worthy of the ululations of a mammon of millionaires.

PASSION'S STORMY KNIGHTS (Foreign Markets)
by Barbara Cartland

As night fell, twisting its ebony foot on the stairway to the sky, the CEO of Spain's Black Knight Ltd. harnessed the stallions of market forces under the whip of his demand. Nothing would stop his fierce, probing interest in Tainted Lily Parfumerie, even as Lily shopped in the Eurodollar market. Her lush trust revenues lured him onward while he pictured her generous supply curve with accruing interest.

But his rapacious love was not to be. For even as Lily's luscious lips attempted, in desperation, to swallow a poison pill, OmniBux's

(cont.)

White Knight subsidiary (with a phalanx of middle managers) arrived as if on silver wings to bestow our tender offer with interest rate sensitivity.

Straining to release the shackles of corporate bonds, Lily embraced the soft, warm body of opinion and, ignoring inherent risks in our loan portfolio, developed mutual fiduciary trust. The honeyed tongues of Olympus were as naught compared to the musky utterances of our currency swap agreement. "Nothing can divide us now," swore White Knight. "We are as one in profits, personnel, and pension plans."

"Again this rapture," sighed Tainted Lily, as she leveraged herself to her gap position. Then, dismissing thoughts of softening demand and non-performing assets, White Knight and his Lily slipped their six-column figures between the silken spread sheets.

His cash flow surged. She held to maturity. The merger was complete.

☙

Research, *Creativity and Other Suspicious Behavior*

I love annual reports. On rainy days my kids spend hours cutting out the pictures.

A creative person can make what seems irrelevant, relevant. That's why he's such a pain in the butt.

A long letter from the CEO tells you he's got too much time on his hands and business stinks.

Stretching research results to make unqualified claims about your product takes the elastic out of your underwear.

Don't use your company's logo on the cover of your annual report unless you want people to identify with it.

Creative people have brains marked "slightly irregular."

✏ ✏

I WORKED AS A WAITER TO SUPPORT MYSELF as an artist. I knew my abstracts would sell, if people would only stop to look at them. Suddenly my paintings started selling as fast as the potato pancakes. The secret to my success? My manager agreed to hang them in the men's room.

⬤

If you worry about having too many creative people on the job, you can always hire a creative person to solve your problem.

Winning second place as Employee-of-the-Month is fine, assuming there were more than two entries.

I've got a knock-out opening and closing sentence for a blockbuster speech. Now all my secretary has to do is fill in the middle.

The only thing wrong with having nothing to say is saying it.

Watch for the percentage change column in your annual report. Doesn't have one? Oops!

We always kept this business in the black, even when we had to borrow money to do it.

An 82-year-old client called me: "I finally got an annual report that was clear and concise. Sell my stock."

When you are looking at the graphs, be sure you're holding your annual report right side up.

Starting from scratch is easier when the scratch is $20 million.

Dealing with the Russians will require patience, contacts, and a whole lot of vodka.

Thirty-nine percent of all CEOs in the United States write their own annual report letter. The rest are written by consultants faking sincerity.

The best way to reduce stress is to make a profit.

At our new company headquarters, the only way to return to where you came in is to wade across the reflecting pool.

Our products are built to last but not forever.

Saying "Let's innovate" is like saying "Let's have sex." In both cases you need a motivated work force.

It's easy to discover a new product. The hard part is figuring out what it is.

It's not a good sign if the janitor is
the only one with work to do after
a brainstorming session.

WHEN I MUSTERED OUT OF THE SERVICE in California in 1960, my replacement was a bright Japanese-American whose father manufactured cars. One day he offered me a ride.

As an engineer, I was surprised. "I'm really impressed. This car is well built. What do you call it?"

"A Toyopet."

"Never heard of it."

"Actually, the company is called Toyota, and this is one of only two cars in the U.S. right now. My father is lining up dealerships. Hey, we could offer you the exclusive distributorship for the whole state of Georgia."

"No, thanks, " I said, trying to be polite. I went home and told my wife, "What kind of crazy person is he, thinking Americans will buy Japanese cars?"

CHAPTER 7

You Think You Were Testy Before?

(It's Time for a Coffee Break)

It's tough to be productive when those office machine hoards rattle your cage on their way to the coffee machine. You know who we mean— characters like the computer hog, the supply moocher, and the moaning martyr who greets you with a bottle of Maalox and his daily complaint.

Walk the halls with us to the coffee machine and see if you recognize some familiar faces.

THE MOOCHER

This scavenger will pick your desk clean.

COMPUTER HOG

He just sits there with an "Apple" in his face.

THE TOXIC WASTE DUMP

The final resting place for green coffee.

STICKÚM NOTE WRITERS

Type A's write so small it must be enlarged on the copier before it is legible.

Type B's start writing LARGE and it gets smaller and smaller.

OFFICE GRAPEVINE

Upper management should strive to develop lines of communications as efficient as the office grapevine.

(It's time for a coffee break.)

Ever mutter to yourself, "How am I ever going to get anything done around here?" You've probably just had *another* half-hour update from the hall-walker as he delivers juicy tidbits of gossip fresh from the employee grapevine.

So if you want to know if you've got what it takes to survive, grab that cup of coffee, jump in the elevator, jam the stop button and take this quiz recently developed by the brain-busting Omnibux research team.

The OMNIBUX Productivity Quiz
for Secretaries & Other People Who REALLY Run Things

1. Which work philosophy is closest to yours?
   a) *Lena Horne:* "Always be smarter than the people who hire you."
   b) *Robert Benchley:* "Anyone can do any amount of work, provided it isn't the work he is supposed to be doing at that moment."
   c) *Robert Frost:* "The reason why worry kills more people than work is that more people worry than work."

2. Time management increases productivity. So how many things can you do efficiently at once?
   a) One. I can only row a boat with one oar (my father was a passive aggressive).

b) Two. I can return phone calls while I take dictation (my mother had twins).

c) Three. I can type meeting notes with one hand, grab a sandwich with the other and distract Fenwick, the time management consultant, simultaneously (my grandfather was a one-man band).

3. An administrative assistant has to be an expert in diplomacy. What does diplomacy mean to you?

a) Listening patiently to the vice-president of marketing who thinks he knows what the average housewife wants even though he's been married to two heiresses and a staff sergeant.

b) Silently ignoring the boss's son, Norton, as he plans the annual shareholders' meeting even though last year he forgot to proofread the proxies proclaiming a 21-1 stock split.

c) Watching helplessly as the product engineer sinks another million dollars into developing a zig-zag zipper.

4. Productivity feeds on creativity. What is the best caption for this drawing?

a) Martin, why are you always on edge?

b) I'll never fit into that parking space.

c) Shirley, quit hiding your locus.

5. Your favorite country & western song is . . .
   a) "Signed, Sealed, and Delivered."
   b) "The Last Thing I Needed First Thing This Morning."
   c) "Take This Job and Shove It."

6. Cultivating outside interests increases productivity. Your favorite activity is . . .
   a) playing tennis.
   b) playing bridge.
   c) playing possum.

7. Your favorite company program is. . .
   a) the employee wellness program.
   b) the employee incentive program.
   c) Sesame Street.

8. Keeping the wheels turning at your job is like . . .
   a) piloting the SST from New York to Paris—quick, easy, and exciting.
   b) driving a '55 Chevy convertible through Manhattan during rush hour in a blizzard.
   c) trying to navigate an American sailboat across the Indian Ocean with a Hungarian crew.

9. The secretary of the future will need to . . .
   a) be well versed in law, marketing and finance.
   b) convey a strong sense of vision and ethics.
   c) know how to say "Yes, boss" in Japanese.

10. You handle conflicts among the sales staff by . . .
    a) requiring written summaries, rebuttals, and reviews.
    b) stepping in directly to make the situation sort of homey.
    c) blocking their FAX access until they stop whining.

11. Productive secretaries must be ruthless in avoiding time-wasting
    salespeople who intrude on tight schedules. You deal with them by . . .
    a) putting on your coat and hat.
    b) sealing all openings to your office.
    c) saying the boss is contagious.

12. How do you control worry?
    a) I hesitate, procrastinate, and ruminate.
    b) I ignore reality.
    c) I cry from 10:30-11:00 each morning.

13. How organized is your desk?
    a) A place for everything and everything in its place.
    b) A place for everything and everything someplace.
    c) I haven't seen my blotter since 1963.

14. Your goal is to become . . .
    a) secretary to an executive.
    b) secretary to the CEO.
    c) Secretary of State.

SCORING:
Give yourself: 9 points for each (a), 5 points for each (b), 0 points for each (c).

RESULTS:
0-37 points: The CLOWNS among you are lots of laughs, perpetual movement but few results. You've learned how to dazzle the world with a well-stocked desk, a permanent smile, and some fancy footwork, helping you to finish your performance before the elephant drops a souvenir on your floppy red feet.

37-85 points: As an ACROBAT, your skills are in great demand. You manage to juggle three books, two computer hard drives, and a flaming chainsaw without slicing your boss's profits.

86-126 points: The top scores put you in the RINGMASTER elite. Your high productivity helps you direct activities in all three rings at once, hold the tigers at bay, and keep the half-man-half-woman faced the right way at all times.

THREE RING CIRCUS

CHAPTER 8

Take My CEO . . . *PLEASE*

(Reflections of the Inscrutable Thirty-Year Man)

The phone call stung his ears like a swarm of killer bees. Banging down the receiver, the executive's brain froze in fear as the impact of the news rippled across every synapse in his pinstriped body: He, Farnsworth Lynley "Bobo" Chadwick, CEO of OmniBux Inc., had been selected as this year's "honoree" at the Ninth Annual Save the Byways Not the Highways Charity Roast.

You think roasts are funny? Don't make us laugh. Fundraisers hoodwink you, use your name, and insult you to raise money for a worthy cause. And you, their sacrificial lamb, are supposed to sit there and smile while they skewer, lambaste and rip you apart, not unlike a roomful of laughing hyenas in a feeding frenzy. Okay, okay, so who wouldn't delight in frying a colleague under the guise of humor?

"Bobo has no equals. Superiors, yes . . ."

"For years I've been rewarded at OmniBux with money and promotions. And to think I owe it all to the morning I saw Bobo coming out of the Pinetar Motel on Route 66 . . ."

"Bobo's amazing. The older he gets, the better a football player he was in college . . ."

What's a sitting duck to do when the heat's turned up during an all-out verbal assault at a one-hundred-dollar-a-plate roast? It's time for a two-week survival course at the UNLISTED ACADEMY OF GUERRILLA HUMOR AND VERBAL DEFENSE.

There, surrounded by experts in Togakure Nin-joke-su, you can immerse yourself in comedic tactics until you can outflank wisecrackers with "tap, rack, and bang" maneuvers, slay foes with razor-sharp wit, and spit out deadly, bevel-edged jokes with machine-gun precision.

"The thing about a roast is your colleagues try to cut you down to their size . . ."

"We all know Frank's spending habits. But he has all the money he'll ever need . . . if he dies by 4 o'clock . . ."

"Patti, you were never funnier. And it's a shame . . ."

The Unlisted Technique demands practice. But mastery will bring skills such as using humor to disarm the enemy, firing potshots on your trusty Remington Manual 1100, dodging the butt end of a double-barreled pun, camouflaging punchlines, and zinging assailants with the subtlety of a Marcel Marceau stealth bomber.

"They don't make them like Harry anymore. Thank God."

Humor is the weapon of the underdog, defused only by guerrilla warfare. On your first day you "men of irony" will be issued a survival kit containing quips and chains, cutting remarks, quartz movement jokes for perfect timing, laughing gas masks, infra-red sarcasm sensors, a map of company loyalties, plastic explosive laughter, faux pas on a rope, a veil of secrecy, and a pork-pie hat.

For the daily nine-mile hike you'll strap twenty-seven pounds of joke books to your back, dodge verbal grenades, sidestep banana peels, and scramble under wired barbs through a field of dirty jokes. In the clearings, snipers hide in trees dropping lines.

"Bobo flunked out of college his freshman year, so he is complimented when anybody calls his speeches sophomoric."

"I know you want to hear the latest dope from headquarters. Well, here he is!"

Next, your commando-in-chief will escort you to the simulation room. While dropouts watch remedial videotapes of The Three Stooges, you and your cohorts will position yourselves in front of the 105 mm Ho-Ho-Howitzer Duelatron Robotic Flamethrower, which fires automatic insults like a tennis ball machine. "Scoutmaster," as it is known by those who know, pauses ten seconds for your deadpan rejoinder and then resumes its barrage of slashing taunts. "I'm here to free the oppressed masses of OmniBux from the joke of sarcastic imperialism." The day ends around the campfire singing the UNLISTED Alma Mater, "Don't Satire Under the Apple Tree With Anyone Else But Me."

By the thirteenth day you'll have mastered the Ten Rules of Guerrilla Humor:

1. A good offensive joke is the best defense.
2. Ally yourself with the mercenaries (paid emcees).
3. When someone knock-knocks, don't answer.
4. When you rappel down the precipice of good taste, it's easy to lose your grip.
5. Off brands of jokes can backfire in your face. Use at your own risk.
6. Blast your target at close range with high caliber jokes.
7. Ad libs are funnier if you practice them first.
8. Shoes pinch, death hurts, humor kills.
9. Never leave home without your silencer for hecklers:
    "Sir, when your IQ reaches 90, sell."
10. Just kidding.

For the final exam, you'll read aloud a document absolving the school from responsibility for your life and then, in the time honored slide-for-life tradition, zoom one hundred feet down a cable onto the stage in front of a ravenous audience.

As you stand there, part of an elite farce of highly trained bombers, smile. The only thing gosh-awful-er than being asked to be the honoree at a roast is never being asked at all.

Reflections *of the Inscrutable Thirty-Year Man*

If you're a salesperson working on commission, you must learn to be comfortable living on the brink of terror.

Getting to this president's chair took me a lot of hard work, which is even harder to accomplish without talent.

A freshly-minted MBA is a good hors d'oeuvre at any business lunch.

I understand the limitations of my job. That's why I don't do anything.

The secret of my success was that no one knew I was there until I retired.

Nobody ever forgets where he buried the hatchet.

My business was always the Reform School for Relatives.

If you're smart, you'll never ask your employees, "What business do you think we're in?"

When people laugh at your joke and it isn't funny, you must be the boss.

Just when you think you've given your all to the company they ask you to donate blood.

A CEO should have vice-presidents he can recognize on sight.

I view my retirement as leaving a job opening for two in an office for one.

WHEN GERT'S GRANDCHILDREN CAME for a visit, they always worked in her restaurant. When Gert retired, they fondly remembered, "Grandma was the only employer we ever had who made us do two hours of work for ten hours of pay."

If you are ever interviewed by the press, look intelligent, use plain English, and never mention your company if you're being indicted.

Money talks, especially when you exceed your credit and someone says, "Hold it, Buster."

My epitaph will read, "I finally got away."

Never give your secretary a present she'll be forced to wear to work and pretend she likes.

It takes hard work to remain incompetent at your job when you've been there for over ten years.

BORED WITH RETIREMENT after being a medical school administrator for thirty years, Bill became a home termite inspector. He figured the few rats he encountered in some basements were tame compared with some of his former deans.

❧   ❧

You know a school is financially sound when they honor an alumna who's taken a vow of poverty.

Working in a man's world wouldn't be bad if you didn't have to work with men.

If you rest on your laurels, all you'll end up with is a leafy design on your behind.

The reason retired military do so well in business is that they've learned to salute the uniform and not the person.

If you really want to know how busy you are, go out of town, call your office, and try to make an appointment with yourself.

A retirement surprise party is in bad taste when you don't know you're retiring.

When a colleague retires, it is not considered good form to snatch his chair while he's still in it.

Fear of hell is not a bad way
to run a business.

Don't wear the old school tie if you flunked out of the old school.

Managing is like making love. No one will admit they're lousy at it.

It's lonely at the top, but there's a hell of a lot of room.

Some people never miss an opportunity to miss an opportunity.

You want to stop having fun? Do away with your competition.

Why is it that the people who do the most work are scrunched together at the bottom of the organization chart?

As AN EXPERT IN MY FIELD, I speak to many groups around the country, and sometimes conventioneers tape my talk for future reference. At a large meeting in Mississippi, I was told that a local businessman preceding me was also an excellent speaker. They were right. I was mesmerized by his words.

Then the host introduced me: "We can't wait to hear what you have to say." I rose, approached the podium, replied, "You just did," and sat down. My predecessor had just delivered my speech, word for word.

CHAPTER 9

Sometimes Bad Acoustics Are a Blessing

(On the Lam at Conventions and Workshops)

Take a group of people with a common interest, such as wanting to get out of town, find a town willing to have them, and—"shazam"—you have the makings of a professional conference.

The difference between a convention and a conference is that a convention only requires its members to assemble periodically, but at a conference you have to listen to people talk. And there's a lot of talk. Mostly about their exciting, challenging technical work. They report on "what we do, how we do it, and why."

Attending a conference and talking about work is always better than being left back at the office to do it. So since all conferences are essentially the same, pick one which meets in a city you want to visit. Next, send for a convention program and, with a straight face, convince the boss the company benefits by your going to Las Vegas for a week.

The program will give you all the necessary information: a file number for your discount airfare, a hotel reservation card, and the time of the complimentary luau. Mail in a registration form to alert the meeting planners, so they'll have your convention packet waiting for you at the registration desk . . . along with your badge. This official badge will let you know which conference you are attending, which company you work for, and how you are really supposed to spell your name.

While the cheery registration volunteer retypes your official badge, you will have plenty of time to examine the contents of your packet. Inside are promotional materials from restaurants, a pad of paper, a pencil embossed with "Buy a Used Car from Clyde's Car-O-Rama" and a key ring donated by Banker's Fiscal Trust in case you want to open an account in a strange new place.

It's now time to decide which of the three kinds of conference meetings to sit in on: workshops, paper sessions, or symposia. At a workshop you will be expected to take notes, look intelligent, and sit still. At a paper session—depending on your particular business—scientists, salespeople, FBI agents, or hairdressers can report on how they compare, investigate, evaluate, measure, explore, review, analyze, select, forecast but never guess about what they do on the job. And at a symposium different people give opinions on "Where are we going now that we are here," "How we got there," and "Now what?"

To entice an audience, papers often have intriguing titles such as, "The Erotic Stimuli of Teeming Management," or "Hostile Takeovers . . . a Million Buds Have Bloomed." The scientist, FBI operative, or hairdresser from Cut-and-Shoot, Texas, might talk on "A Romp with Anti-inflammatory Agents."

After selecting your meeting, find the room where it will be held. For starters, most meeting rooms are called salons, and the meeting will probably be in Salon A, Salon B, Salon AB, or Salon BA . . . unless it's been moved to a room with a theme name.

Theme monikers often depend on the host city or the interior decorator's fanciful imagination. In Detroit you might meet in The Converter Slag Room, The Abrasive Blasting Room, or The Combustion Chamber. Unless the decorator has his way, in which case you may need a field guide to sight The Fulvous Tree Duck Room.

If the meeting begins on time, as many as five papers can be presented comfortably. This arrangement ensures that at least five people will have to sit through the entire session.

The paper presenters usually sit behind a long steel table with their backs to a solid wall to protect them from their colleagues in the audience. A sixth person will preside. There are only three kinds of presiders: those who can tell time, those who can't, and those who can be bribed to allow only thirty seconds at the end of the meeting for the audience's insightful questions.

To enhance a paper presentation, at least one person will use an overhead projector, thus affording the opportunity to get acquainted with your fellow attendees while the presenter rearranges the slides, replaces the bulb, and runs around looking for an extension cord.

People who attend paper sessions fall into five categories:

1. The obsessive-compulsive who arrives twenty minutes early for an 8:00 a.m. meeting and wonders, "Where is everybody?"

2. The conference nomad who wanders in twenty minutes late, kicks six folding chairs, sits down, asks loudly, "What did I miss," stays ten minutes and then saunters out again.

3. The good buddies who sit together, chat loudly about old times, and always act surprised when it's time to leave.

4. The scholar who comes armed with a lengthy statement he hopes will pass for a question.

5. And the inquisitor who sits on the edge of a chair, ready to pounce with, "Would you run those numbers by us again and give me the name, rank, and serial number of the person who taught you to count?"

The paper session is over when nobody claps but everyone leaves. Now there's a choice: go to another meeting or relocate to The Wazoo Club up the road. If it's up to Wazoo—well, folks, you've finally found the real stuff meetings are made of. Let's call it "nitty-gritty networking."

On the Lam at Conventions and Workshops

You can always spot the meeting planner. She's the one who looks as if a vampire has been sucking on her neck.

✐ ✐ ✐

LATE FOR A FLIGHT FROM DULUTH to a conference in Minneapolis, I arrived just in time to dash aboard. Buckling up, I noticed I was the only passenger on the 737 jet, with 7 flight attendants. After take-off I surreptitiously got permission to use the microphone: "Attention, flight crew, this is your passenger speaking. . ."

✐

When presenting a paper, stare sincerely into people's foreheads.

If you're a really good speaker, no one will care what you are saying.

✐ ✐

A lively discussion should involve more than one person.

As KEYNOTE SPEAKER AT A CONVENTION, I couldn't be late, but desperation set in as I spent forty-five harrowing minutes searching in vain for a downtown parking spot. I finally arrived just in time for my speech. Out of five hundred people, I was the only woman there who missed lunch, talked for an hour, and paid $29.95 for an oil and lube job I didn't need.

Presiding over the yearly planning meeting at my bank is like walking into a rattlesnake roundup with bare feet and juicy, fat frogs between my toes.

An executive wilderness experience means going into the woods and doing things with all the people you'd never do them with at the office.

When a guy gets drunk and slaps you on the back at a convention, he's glad to see you. When he shakes your hand, he's looking for a job.

I don't have to go into the wilderness to practice
team behavior in a hostile environment.

There's something about relaxing that makes me very nervous.

At Caesar's Palace in Las Vegas where I tend bar, a conventioneer in his eighties consumed three bourbons. Suddenly clutching his chest in pain, he collapsed and was rushed to the hospital, where the nurse cured his "heart attack" by unbuttoning his shirt and removing the open pin on his conventioneer's badge.

Always let your audience know that you are coming to the end of your paper so they can pretend they were listening.

When I asked a fellow conventioneer to spell his name, he said, "Merrill, as in Merrill Lynch, without the money." And his wife added, "But with all the bull."

"Standing room only" means the meeting was scheduled in the men's room, and three people showed up.

If the workshop starts before my partner gets there, you know it's starting on time.

I know my church is modernizing, but the seminary didn't prepare me for attending a workshop for clergy titled, "Doing Evangelism in a Negative Congregational Climate."

It takes alot of bull elephants
to make an ivory tower.

As a six-foot-six foreign service officer, I was delighted with the friendliness at my Asian post. By the end of an evening I was always surrounded by an animated group. I was devastated to learn the key to my popularity. Apparently at the beginning of these large gatherings, couples would say, "When it's time to go, I'll meet you next to the tall American."

CHAPTER 10

Who Killed Speling?

(And Other Mysteries At Work)

The eerie silence was broken only by the pounding of a fist against the window, incessant at first, frantic. Then the unanswered plea faded into the night until finally only the echo remained.

Next morning the body was discovered—a wizened, pathetic soul who, after valiantly surviving innumerable attacks, finally choked to death on a bowl of alphabet soup. Evidence points to many suspects. But who really killed "Spelling?"

Consider the clues. Walk into any grocery store and examine the shelves: Ziploc Sandwich Bags, Luv's Disposable Diapers, Kool-Aid. Or have dinner at Chick-fil-A, Chopstix, or Dunkin' Donuts (a double whammy). In a hurry? Perhaps you'd prefer a stop at the Majik Market, Krispy Kreme Doughnuts, or a U-Tote-M.

A host of murder suspects lurk in the advertising-industrial-educational complex, and it's time they were unmasked.

Suspect #1: Education. Students primed on computers write "secratary," "seperate," or "allready."

The problem is compounded by slang and colloquialisms creeping into compositions. "Gonna" will someday be a bona fide word, conjugated alongside "to be": I'm gonna, you're gonna, he, she, or it's gonna. When this generation of students is unleashed on the English-speaking world, you'd better guard your diphthongs with your life.

So let's turn to *suspect #2:* Advertising. To develop product names that can become registered trademarks, ad execs murder letters. Thus consumers can buy

Roach-Pruf, Nestle's Quik, and D-Zerta. As for yoghurt, it lost its "h" as soon as it became trendy. Vestigial letters lie awake, lest an adman kidnap them some starless night and sell them on the black market to Sesame Street.

In the meantime, it's already too late for I-G-H-T, the dodo bird of spelling. Consider Lite Beer, Sleep EZY Nite Lites (a triple whammy) and, perhaps the worse mangling of all, Nytol tablets. Out of eight correct letters, Bristol-Myers managed to salvage only three. How much longer can bologna hold out?

Suspect #3: Business has also behaved abominably. Stride-Rite corrupts our children's spelling in their formative years, abetted by Playskool Toys and Toys R' Us. Then they munch Chex cereal in four flavors of misspellings and dine at Cap'N Pegs.

But before the verdict, the defense asserts that spelling reform is not all bad. Would Napoleon Buonaparte have been such a despot had he not been driven crazy by constantly having to explain, "No, no, that's B as in battle, U as in udder . . ." And who could blame Ulysses for leaving home, with a spelling burden like that?

The suspects are all guilty, no doubt a conspiracy.

If this is the future, why not get in step and rewrite the past as well? We could start with The Constitushun, The Bill of Rites, and The Deklarashun of 'Ndependens. Rite on.

But spelling is only one of the . . .

When you work in doorless cubicles, where do you go when you need to scratch?

Why is there always one jackass who has to ask, "What is your recommendation?"

Whenever we meet at a round table, I arrive early so I won't have to guess who's in charge.

There have been so many takeovers here, when I leave the office, I tell my secretary, "If my boss calls—find out his name."

✎ ✎ ✎

SOON AFTER MY FRIEND TEDDY GURSHINSKI became president of his company, I heard a rumor that he had changed his name. "Aha!" I sneered, "Another person who wants to hide his ethnic origin." A week later I received a letter from him proudly signed, "Sincerely yours, Gary Gurshinski."

✎

"She can't come to the phone, she's in a meeting," might mean she really is in a meeting.

You want to baffle the competition? Pay your bills on time.

It tells you something when one incompetent employee doesn't stand out in the crowd.

What can you say to a customer who walks into your hardware store and asks, "Do you have a yardstick that is four feet long?"

Boarding a single-engine plane with five seats, seven pieces of luggage and the chairman of the board is no time to lie about your weight.

My mentor always says, "No pain, no gain." But why pre-pay?

Never ponder the meaning of corporate life.

✐   ✐

AFTER GETTING THE RUNAROUND from a customer's book-keeper, a credit manager at Mid-continent Agencies, Inc. insisted on speaking to Mr. "Jones," a part owner. The bookkeeper apologized: "That's impossible. Mr. 'Jones' is in jail." When he then asked to speak to the other partner, Mr.

IF you have a tough problem, ask your boss. He will always know which secretary can solve it.

"Smith," the exasperated bookkeeper said, "That's impossible, too. Mr. 'Jones' is in jail for shooting Mr. 'Smith.'"

When a customer phoned and asked, "Do you have a crockery dog bowl with a blue stripe on the top and the bottom that says D O G on it?" I answered, "Yes, we have it in stock." And she said, "Great! What does it look like?"

As a young country doctor in Texas, I always admired other businesspeople who framed their first dollar, but how do you nail a live chicken to the wall?

Nobody misspells v-a-c-a-t-i-o-n.

My boss can't make a decision, shrieks when excited, and goes to a hair stylist once a week. But why doesn't anyone ever say, "Just like a man?"

Who will pour coffee again now that our workshop leader lost control of our assertiveness training group?

Want to know the only two ways to advance in business? Make decisions. Avoid decisions.

It's amazing what a good idea it is, when your boss thinks he thought of it first.

Our Chief Information Officer is living proof that there is such a thing as artificial intelligence.

⌘   ✎   ✎

MY BOSS, MR. DOOLEY, EXPECTED to be served with a subpoena, so he instructed me to tell the sheriff's deputy he was out of town. Every day for three weeks, the deputy arrived, rang the bell at the reception desk, and listened to my daily fib. Each day Mr. Dooley watched out the window as he drove off.

On the twenty-second day, the ritual was repeated. Ten minutes after the deputy drove off, he returned, quietly tiptoed through the receptionist's door to the back hall, and sang out, "YOO-hoo, Mr. DOO-ley," to which Mr. Dooley trilled, "WHA-at?" He was tied up in court for six months.

It's Hard to Pull Yourself Up
by Your Bootstraps When You're Naked

(Clues for Rookies)

Ladies, gentlemen and graduates. As dean of your college, it is an honor for me to present today's commencement speaker, J. Van Muggenrun, an eminently successful business leader whose reputation has not yet been tainted in the public eye. The brass plaque on his solid mahogany door says, "Chairman of the Board of OmniBux." Here in our marketing department we know him affectionately as "Muggs," our benefactor and donor of the first $100,000 Folding Chair of Business Ethics. Without further ado, please give him your rapt attention . . .

Thank you, Dean Wylie. As I look around these hallowed halls at you graduates—diplomas in one hand, resumes in the other—I am reminded of my dear, departed mother, who on my graduation day whispered, "Son, always remember that King Richard stabbed the other king in the tower before he smothered the babies. Business before pleasure!"

Not only did I take her words to heart that day, but I never forgot the way she said them. At that moment she entrusted the Muggenrun fortune to me, and I vowed never to let her down. Only when I took over the family business did I realize the sacrifices made by great-great-grandfather Muggenrun, who started with a small resale shoe business in Boot Hill, Arizona, invested his money in candle snuffers, and ended up in Chapter 11 with wick burns and a singed mustache. It was his meager life insurance that provided the capital that Grandfather used to seed OmniBux.

Soon you graduates will march out in cadence, tassles dangling from your flat hats, ready to test the principles you learned in this great institution. Until now, your work has been directed by trained professorial minds, but tomorrow you must rely on your own efforts. In plain English, you have invested a fortune in your education, so now make it pay off.

There are only three things you have to remember:

1) Any job you want is yours unless there's another applicant.
2) The average American interviewer needs six feet of space between you and him.
3) And whatever you do, lean toward the interviewer at a 45-degree angle, listen, and look concerned.

Once hired, you will soon learn if your courses apply in today's corporate climate. Will geometry help you produce credible rows of figures for skeptical stockholders? Will abnormal psychology get you through the stress of volatile capital movements? And did your philosophy course teach you enough about the "shades of grey" phenomenon? Personally, I learned how to be fiscally fit from running track, always jumping over the bottom line.

Many of you will end up in personnel, marketing or sales. But businesses aren't static, they are merely a collection of changing problems. When you solve one, you change the organization. And the minute you change the organization, your job is in jeopardy. So it's up to you either to invent new problems or delegate problem-solving to your subordinates. That way you'll keep your job and become an administrator.

It's a balance between solving problems and avoiding solving problems. That's what work is all about. That, and balancing the books. If you can't balance the books, use your kid's charge account to handle the deficit, the good old American way.

As we approach the twenty-first century, the root of many difficulties lies in the inability of companies to convince consumers that certain activities are not only appropriate but justified. For instance:

—In our free enterprise system, it's good business to entertain customers and add the cost to our product price. After all, the motto of this great university, "In Vino Veritas," emphasizes the importance we all place on the business lunch.

—Businesses that want to succeed must support the community by donating to charitable causes such as the Anti-tenting Society for the Protection of Termites and Other Essential Boring Wildlife. Again, it's fine and dandy to pass the cost to the consumer.

So what else determines the price of our goods? There's advertising, packaging, marketing and, of course, our compensation package with enough perks to keep top line executives humming. And last but not least . . . all the remedial training courses that $45,000 of graduate school did not provide.

By the way, if your company handles defense contracts, most of the business practices I just mentioned are "iffy," so it's best to charge $700 for a ballpeen hammer up front and to hell with the nuances.

As long as the price is right, there'll be plenty of economic opportunity for each of you. Just keep faith in the free market. Keep your eyes on the world. Keep your face lifted. Keep your money in the Bahamas.

So what if Japan is coming?

So what if Europe is coming?

Go for it!

But, graduates, before you get there, I recommend that first you take off those silly robes.

Clues for Rookies

My style is unprofessional. I never went to college, and I'm not full of personality. But I'm the owner, we're making a fortune, and nobody ever asks to see my SAT scores.

An entrepreneur is someone who works twenty hours a day, has no social life, suffers chronic fatigue, finds business books sexy, and says, "Hey, work is really fun!"

You know an alumnus has fallen from grace when his alma mater removes his portrait from its walls and doesn't send a thank you note for his $10 million donation.

Never ask why your predecessor left the job unless you can upgrade your threshold for pain.

A full-time job is a lot of work.

Trying to get ahead in someone else's family-owned business is a lot like panning for sand.

N-e-v-e-r date the manager of your company credit union.

Let the title go and take the cash.

The quickest way to get your boss's undivided
attention is to mispronounce her name.